Megan McDonald

My Favorite Writer

Tatiana Tomljanovic

WEIGL PUBLISHERS INC.

Published by Weigl Publishers Inc.
350 5th Avenue, Suite 3304, PMB 6G
New York, NY 10118-0069

Website: www.weigl.com

Library of Congress Cataloging-in-Publication Data

Tomljanovic, Tatiana.
Megan McDonald : my favorite writer / Tatiana Tomljanovic.
    p. cm.
Includes index.
ISBN 978-1-59036-928-9 (hard cover : alk. paper) -- ISBN 978-1-59036-
929-6 (soft cover : alk. paper)
 1. McDonald, Megan--Juvenile fiction. 2. Novelists, American--20th
century--Biography--Juvenile literature. I. Title.
  PS3563.A2864Z89 2008
  813'.54--dc22
  [B]
                                        2008003971

Printed in the United States of America
1 2 3 4 5 6 7 8 9 0 12 11 10 09 08

Project Coordinator
Heather C. Hudak

Design
Terry Paulhus

All of the Internet URLs given in the book were valid at the time of
publication. However, due to the dynamic nature of the Internet, some
addresses may have changed, or sites may have ceased to exist since
publication. While the author and publisher regret any inconvenience this
may cause readers, no responsibility for any such changes can be accepted
by either the author or the publisher.

Contents

Megan McDonald

MILESTONES

1959 Born February 28 in Pittsburgh, Pennsylvania

1969 Sees her name in print for the first time on a story she wrote for her school newspaper

1973 Gets her first job as a page, shelving books, at a public library

1981 Graduates from Oberlin College with a degree in children's literature

1982 Meets Katherine Paterson, her favorite children's author

1986 Graduates from the University of Pittsburgh with a master of **library science** degree

1990 Publishes her first book, *Is This a House for a Hermit Crab?*

1993 Publishes her first novel, *The Bridge to Nowhere*

1994 Marries Richard Haynes on September 22

2000 Publishes her first Judy Moody book

2003 Wins the First Annual Beverly Cleary Children's Choice Award for Judy Moody

2007 Publishes *Meet Julie*, a series of American Girl books

Megan McDonald is a comedienne. She likes to make other people, especially children, laugh. Almost all of Megan's books are funny. She has written more than 30 children's books, including picture books and chapter books.

The Judy Moody chapter books for young readers is Megan's most popular series. Judy Moody is a loud, opinionated third grader who has many different moods—good moods and bad moods. Judy has a younger brother, Stink, who she enjoys playfully tormenting.

Over the years, Megan's Judy Moody books have become so popular that she has written books about Judy's brother Stink as well. The Judy Moody books have made many bestseller lists, reaching millions of readers across the world. The books are printed in many different languages, including Japanese and Latvian.

The ideas for Megan's books come from her own experiences growing up. "Sometimes," Megan writes on her web site, "I think I am Judy Moody." As a writer, Megan is always on the lookout for a new story idea.

Early Childhood

"In everything there is story—a leaf falling, the smell of cinnamon, a dog that looks both ways before crossing the street."
Megan McDonald

Megan Jo McDonald was born February 28, 1959, in Pittsburgh, Pennsylvania, to John McDonald, an ironworker, and Mary Louise McDonald, a social worker. Megan's mom read all the **classic** novels. She was **inspired** to become a social worker after reading Charles Dickens' novel *A Tale of Two Cities* in college. Megan's dad also loved to read.

Both Megan's parents encouraged her to read. Each year at Christmas, Megan's mom went to Kaufman's, a big department store in downtown Pittsburgh. There, she bought Megan and each of her four older sisters a **hardcover** book. Megan read many books growing up, but her favorite was *Harriet the Spy*.

The McDonald house had books piled on tables, spilling off shelves, tucked into pockets, and hiding under beds. Megan learned from an early age never to leave home without a book.

Pittsburgh was founded in 1758.

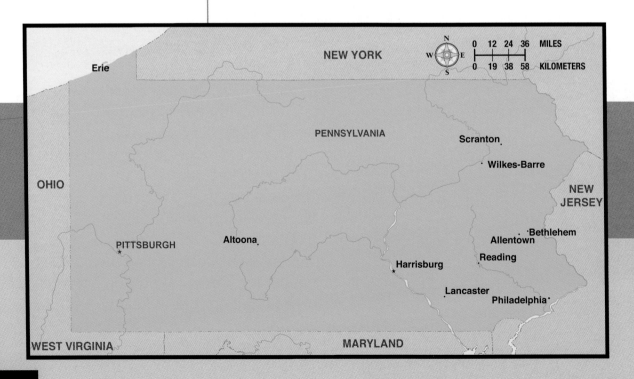

When Megan was not reading, she was playing outdoors with her sisters and best friends from across the street. The McDonald house was surrounded by woods, fields, and a creek. These places were perfect for exploring. Megan spent her summers catching frogs and **centipedes**, searching for nickels that her dad hid inside tree stumps, and building secret hideouts.

Playtime was always interrupted by the dinner bell clanging, calling the girls back home. Megan and her mom and sisters would sit around their large kitchen table and wait for their dad to come home. During dessert, Megan's dad always told a story. His nickname was "Little Johnny the Storyteller." He made up funny and interesting stories based on the most imaginative things. The shape of peanut butter heaped on a Ritz cracker might inspire a story about an enchanted mountain cave. The pattern ice cream made on the lid of a carton might represent a mythical, magical land. He also told stories about his own childhood. These included stories about the **huckster** who would sell potatoes around his neighborhood. The huckster would cry out, "Abba-no potata-man!" This became the inspiration for Megan's book *The Potato Man*.

Megan's father has always been an influential part of her life.

Growing Up

With four older sisters, it was hard for Megan to get a word in edgewise at the dinner table. In elementary school, she began to **stutter**. Megan found it difficult to talk, so her mother bought her a copy of *Harriet the Spy*, along with a spiral notebook. She wanted Megan to express her thoughts and feelings in writing. Megan began to write down all of her thoughts, observations, and experiences, just like her favorite character, Harriet the Spy.

Harriet the Spy was made into a movie starring Rosie O'Donnell and Michelle Trachtenberg.

Although Megan does not know exactly when she began wanting to be a writer, she knows the spiral notebook helped her to think like a writer. When she first got the notebook, she started to watch what happened around her more closely. Megan would write down her observations in her notebook. The first story Megan published was about a pencil sharpener. It was told from the point of view of the pencil sharpener and described what it was like to eat pencil shavings all day. When Megan was in the fifth grade, the story was published in the school newspaper, *The Knight News*. The pencil sharpener was the first story Megan wrote all by herself, without her mom's help. She is very proud of this story and still keeps a copy of it.

Inspired to Write

Megan looks at her surroundings for inspiration for her stories. Something as silly as a pencil sharpener or as scary as a one-eyed potato man can become a good story.

Megan began writing stories at a young age.

After the story of the pencil sharpener was published, Megan wrote a new story every month for her school newspaper. She won an essay contest, and one of her stories was published in *Weekly Reader*, an educational magazine for children.

Megan's mother and sisters were a big influence in her life.

Megan has always been close to her family. At age 10, she had a new nephew.

As Megan continued her schooling, she read more and more books. At 14, she received a job shelving books at the public library. While at her library job, Megan had trouble finishing her daily tasks because she kept looking at the children's picture books. Many librarians noticed Megan's interest in children's books and encouraged her to read aloud to kids at story time, play guitar, sing songs, and put on plays, puppet, and magic shows. Megan made up a comedy routine with her best friend Judy about a magician and her assistant who would mess up the magic tricks. Megan quickly learned that she was good at making children laugh.

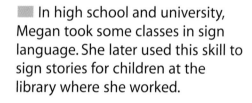 In high school and university, Megan took some classes in sign language. She later used this skill to sign stories for children at the library where she worked.

Favorite Books

Growing up, *Harriet the Spy* was Megan's favorite book. Her all-time favorite children's book writer is Katherine Paterson. Katherine wrote *The Bridge to Terabithia*. When Megan first read *The Bridge to Terabithia* for a children's literature course in college, she cried because the book is very sad.

After she graduated from college, Megan lived in Williamsburg, Virginia. This town was located near Norfolk, Virginia, where Katherine Paterson lived at the time. While in Virginia, Megan attended many of Katherine's book readings and talks. One day, Megan was able to meet the author she so admired in person. Katherine taught Megan that a writer cannot wait for inspiration to happen before beginning to write. A writer must just sit down and begin.

Learning the Craft

After graduating from high school, Megan was accepted into the creative writing program at Oberlin College. She loved her writing classes there, until the day her **professor** called her into his office. He told Megan to rip up all of the poems that she had ever written. He then told her that she was a prose writer. Megan was crushed. She went back to her room and cried and looked up the word "prose" in the dictionary. Prose is defined as writing or speech that is ordinary. Megan did not want to be ordinary, so she began looking for the extraordinary all around her in everyday life. Following her passion, Megan graduated from Oberlin College in 1981 with a degree in children's literature.

After college, Megan was hired for her first real job at a bookstore. She then went on to work at the public library. There, she enjoyed inspiring a love of reading and books in children of all ages.

Megan says, "I spend my days looking at things sideways, upside down, questioning everything, always wanting to see the inside."

As a children's librarian, Megan told stories to children, played her guitar, and sung songs. She learned more about the kinds of stories children liked to hear and what made them laugh. Megan later used some of the stories she made up for the library's story time in her books. Her very first book, *Is This a House for a Hermit Crab?*, is based on a story she told aloud at the library.

While working as a children's librarian, Megan went to graduate school at the University of Pittsburgh. She finished in 1986 with a masters degree in library science. After graduation, Megan took a a leave of absence from her job at the library so that she could write her first book.

Inspired to Write

For Megan, life experiences, such as learning about many different people and settings, helped her become a better writer than many of the writing classes she took in school.

■ Megan worked at the Carnegie Library in Pittsburgh for about four years.

Getting Published

"Sitting in that dark audience, listening to Dick's voice, I started to hear my own voice."
Megan McDonald

Getting published was not a quick or easy process for Megan. It was only after Megan's 31st birthday that her first book made it to print. Although Megan had been writing stories since elementary school, it was when she met Richard, or Dick, Jackson, a children's book editor, that her stories were published in book form.

Megan met Richard Jackson at a festival of children's books held at Carnegie Library. At the festival, many writers and editors, including Richard Jackson, spoke. One of the writers said that an editor's insights helped make her writing much, much better. Megan wanted to know more, so she decided to talk to the editor herself. Richard Jackson invited Megan to send him some of her writing. It took Megan two years to work up the courage to send Richard Jackson the story about the hermit crab. With her editor's help, Megan's books about the hermit crab, the potato man, the bridge to nowhere, and many others were published.

The Publishing Process

Publishing companies receive hundreds of **manuscripts** from authors each year. Only a few manuscripts become books. Publishers must be sure that a manuscript will sell many copies. As a result, publishers reject most of the manuscripts they receive.

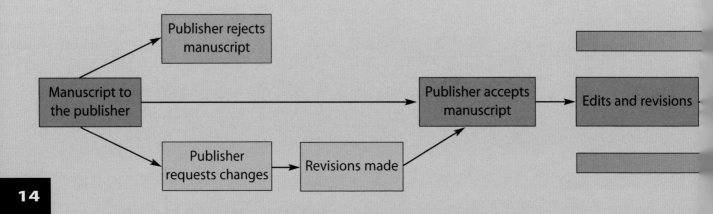

14

Richard has been Megan's editor for more than 20 years. Over time, Megan wrote more books than one editor could help her get ready to publish. She began the search for another editor who might be interested in a new series of stories she was writing about a moody third grader. Megan sent her stories to Mary Lee Donovan at Candlewick Press. Mary Lee loved them. Together, Megan and Mary Lee turned the stories into a short novel, which became the first book of the wildly popular Judy Moody series.

The Judy Moody books were first inspired by Megan's childhood stories of growing up with four sisters. When Megan talked to her readers, they often asked her, "Are you ever in a bad mood? Can you write books when you're in a bad mood?" The idea of bad moods, good moods, happy and sad moods began to take shape as an idea for a story, so Megan made up the character of Judy Moody.

Inspired to Write

For Megan McDonald and many other writers, writing is about finding their inner voice. Telling a good, honest story means being true to yourself and taking risks.

Once a manuscript has been accepted, it goes through many stages before it is published. Often, authors change their work to follow an editor's suggestions. Once the book is published, some authors receive royalties. This is money based on book sales.

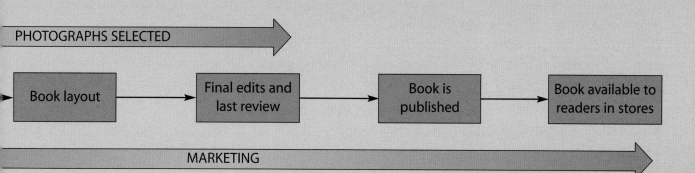

PHOTOGRAPHS SELECTED →

Book layout → Final edits and last review → Book is published → Book available to readers in stores

MARKETING →

Writer Today

Today, Megan lives in Sebastopol, California, with her husband Richard Haynes. Their cozy house, just outside the town, is surrounded by persimmon trees, calla lily, and cosmos flowers. From their front porch, Megan and Richard enjoy watching hummingbirds, egrets, hawks, and families of quail. Regular visitors are a funny flock of 15 wild turkeys.

Richard works as a marriage and family **therapist**. He is also a writer. Megan writes full time and tours the United States and around the world, visiting schools and libraries, and talking to kids about the writing process and her books.

■ Megan enjoys writing from her home office.

Megan continues to write about Judy Moody's hilarious everyday adventures with her younger brother Stink. She works with both her editor, Mary Lee Donovan, and an artist, Peter Reynolds, to bring her books to life. Peter Reynolds is a talented, award-winning illustrator. He draws hundreds of pictures of Judy, Stink, and their friends.

Megan spends her days thinking, imagining, and dreaming up new stories. Sometimes, she thinks like a hermit crab. Other times, she pretends to be a bossy big sister with a younger brother named Stink. Megan says that she is lucky to be a writer because she is able to spend her day imagining new stories, and she can go to work in her pajamas.

Megan's sisters have had a big influence on her writing.

Popular Books

Megan McDonald has written more than eight Judy Moody books. Fans of Judy Moody can get a Judy Moody activity book, and a Mood Journal or a Judy Moody doll at from their local bookstore. This series has inspired stories about other characters. Here are some of Megan's most popular books.

AWARDS

Judy Moody Was In a Mood. Not a Good Mood. A Bad Mood.

American Library Association Notable Children's Book

New York Public Library Best Children's Book: 100 Titles for Reading and Sharing

Publishers Weekly Best Children's Book of the Year

Beverly Cleary Children's Choice Award Winner

Garden State Children's Book Award Winner

Judy Moody Was In a Mood. Not a Good Mood. A Bad Mood.

The very first of the Judy Moody books introduces Judy on her first day of school in the third grade. Judy Moody is not looking forward to the third grade. She knows that her new desk will not have an armadillo sticker with her name on it like her desk in second grade. Her new classroom will not have a porcupine named Roger, and she will probably have to sit in the first row, where her teacher will notice every time she tries to pass a note to her best friend, Rocky. Judy is a moody third grader. She has mad-faced moods, funniest-thing-ever moods, and every other mood you can imagine.

Stink: The Incredible Shrinking Kid

Stink, Judy Moody's younger brother, is 3 feet, 8 inches tall. He is the shortest kid in second grade. Even the class newt is growing faster than Stink. Every morning Judy measures her brother against the Shrimp-O-Meter with her Elizabeth Blackwell Woman of Science ruler. Then one day, Judy measures Stink at three feet, seven and three-quarter inches. Stink is shrinking! Stink tries everything to look taller, but wearing vertical stripes and spiking his hair is not fooling anyone. *Stink: The Incredible Shrinking Kid* is the first of Megan McDonald's Stink books. The book is filled with comic strips drawn by Stink and has many fun facts about Presidents' Day because Stink's hero is James Madison, the shortest president in U.S. history.

Megan decided Stink needed a book of his own after she entered a classroom where the students were chanting, "Stink, Stink, Stink!" Since then, she has written three more books about Stink—*Stink and the Incredible Super Galactic Jawbreaker* and *Stink and the World's Worst Super-Stinky Sneakers*, and *Stink and the Great Guinea Pig Express.*

AWARD

Stink: The Incredible Shrinking Kid

Chicago Public Library Best Book

Buckeye Children's Book Award Winner (Ohio)

Rhode Island Children's Book Award Winner

Judy Moody & Stink The Holly Joliday

Megan's newest book, *The Holly Joliday*, co-stars Judy Moody and Stink in a Christmas adventure. Judy Moody wants presents, presents and more presents, but all her brother Stink wants this year is snow. It has not snowed on Christmas Day in Virginia for more than 100 years. Then, Stink and Judy meet the new mailman, Mr. Jack Frost. He looks like a jolly old elf, likes the cold, and knows a great deal about weather patterns. Stink begins to think that maybe this year will be magical.

Julie Albright—Stories from the Seventies

Julie Albright—Stories from the Seventies is a series of six titles that Megan wrote for the American Girl series of books. American Girl books aim to inspire girls to reach for their dreams and be the best that they can be. Through the tales of girls living at different times in history, the American Girl books share the traditions, culture, and events of these eras. Julie Albright shares what life was like in the United States during the 1970s.

In this series of books, readers learn that Julie's parents have just divorced, and she will be living with her mother, a few miles away from where they lived as a family. Julie is faced with many challenges. In addition to adjusting to her new home life, Julie wants to join the school basketball team, but girls are not allowed to play, her mother is working full-time, and she must leave her best friend, Ivy. In each book, Julie learns how to cope with these challenges and many others.

Creative Writing Tips

Writing can be difficult. Sometimes, the hardest part is getting started. Megan read many books and wrote down plenty of stories before she became a published author. Here are some tips that might help you start writing or become a better writer.

Open Your Eyes

Ideas for stories can come from any place. Most of Megan's story ideas come from real life. She watches the people around her very closely. She notices what they look like, what they do, what they say, and even how things smell. Some of the characters and things that happen in Megan's books are based on Megan's own life, such as the time Judy Moody put a fake hand in the toilet to scare Stink. When Megan was a young child, her family visited Washington, DC. They went on a tour of the White House without her because she was too young. Megan was left at home with her aunt. To play a funny joke on her sisters because they got to go to the White House, Megan put a fake hand in the toilet.

Though Megan did not get to go to the White House with her family, she found ways to have fun at home.

Keep a Notebook

Writing every day is good practice for a writer. Keep a notebook with you at all times, and write down what you see. Megan's mom gave her a spiral notebook when she was young. She wrote in it every day. In your notebook, describe what you see, hear, taste, and smell when doing activities, such as riding the bus or eating breakfast. Try to make up interesting stories about these everyday things. When you describe people and places in detail, readers will experience the story more fully. This makes the story come to life.

Inspired to Write

Writers do not always have a notebook available when they have an idea. If you are inspired to write, grab any scrap piece of paper that is nearby, and jot down your ideas the moment they come to you. Megan often writes the beginning of a book by scribbling notes and ideas on a napkin.

Write Backwards

Sometimes, a writer has an idea for the end of a story rather than the beginning. When Megan heard about a man who drove off an unfinished bridge, she wanted to write a story about it. Megan wanted the story to end with the man going over the unfinished bridge, so she wrote the story backwards. She wrote the end first and then wrote the beginning and middle. Some authors write the end of their stories first. Others write the middle first. They think about what is going to happen in each chapter and then start writing the words and sentences.

Edit

Every good writer has a good editor. Megan needs her editor, Mary Lee, to help make her books better. If possible, ask a teacher, parent, friend, or classmate to read your stories and tell you what they think. Sometimes, a sentence that makes sense to you does not make sense to someone else. Editing makes writing sharp. Try asking more than one person to edit your stories. Make sure to re-read and edit your stories yourself. Read them out loud to make sure they still make sense.

■ Anyone can help edit your writing, including your classmates.

Writing a Biography Review

A biography is an account of an individual's life that is written by another person. Some people's lives are very interesting. In school, you may be asked to write a biography review. The first thing to do when writing a biography review is to decide whom you would like to learn about. Your school library or community library will have a large selection of biographies from which to choose. Are you interested in an author, a sports figure, an inventor, a movie star, or a president? Finding the right book is your first task. Whether you choose to write your review on a biography of Megan McDonald or another person, the task will be similar.

Begin your review by writing the title of the book, the author, and the person featured in the book. Then, start writing about the main events in the person's life. Include such things as where the person grew up and what his or her childhood was like. You will want to add details about the person's adult life, such as whether he or she married or had children. Next, write about what you think makes this person special. What kinds of experiences influenced this individual? For instance, did he or she grow up in unusual circumstances? Was the person determined to accomplish a goal? Include any details that surprised you. A concept web is a useful research tool. Use the concept web on the right to begin researching your biography review.

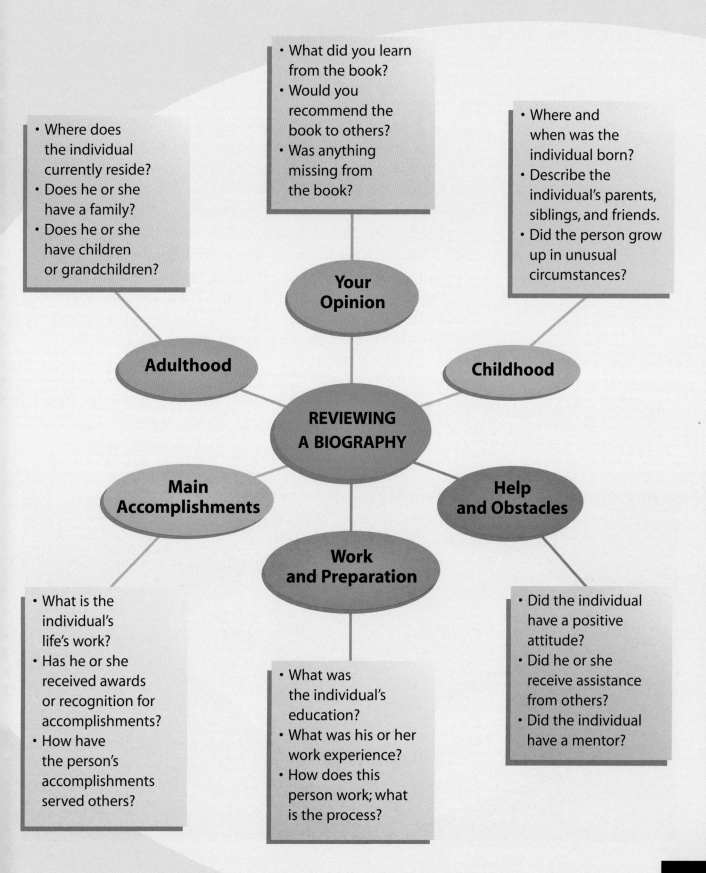

- Where does the individual currently reside?
- Does he or she have a family?
- Does he or she have children or grandchildren?

- What did you learn from the book?
- Would you recommend the book to others?
- Was anything missing from the book?

- Where and when was the individual born?
- Describe the individual's parents, siblings, and friends.
- Did the person grow up in unusual circumstances?

Your Opinion

Adulthood

Childhood

REVIEWING A BIOGRAPHY

Main Accomplishments

Help and Obstacles

Work and Preparation

- What is the individual's life's work?
- Has he or she received awards or recognition for accomplishments?
- How have the person's accomplishments served others?

- What was the individual's education?
- What was his or her work experience?
- How does this person work; what is the process?

- Did the individual have a positive attitude?
- Did he or she receive assistance from others?
- Did the individual have a mentor?

Fan Information

Megan loves to tell stories. She tells stories about her life growing up, hermit crabs, and unfinished bridges. Sometimes, Megan travels across the United States so she can tell stories, talk about her books, and answer questions. She speaks at conferences and attends Judy Moody days whenever she can. Judy Moody days are community events where children dress up like their favorite Judy Moody character, learn about the latest books in the series, and take part in fun activities, such as treasure hunts.

Schools sometimes ask Megan to visit and talk about the writing process. When she does, she brings a slide show featuring photos, newspaper clippings, drawings, rough drafts, edits, sketches, **storyboards**, and even mistakes that she has made when an idea is on its way to becoming a book.

Students can learn more about Megan and her books by visiting Megan's website or the Judy Moody website.

Megan gets a great deal of mail from her fans.

WEB LINKS

Megan's Official Website

www.meganmcdonald.net

Visitors to Megan's official website will learn more about the author, including Ten Things You Didn't Know About Megan McDonald. The site includes activities for children and a virtual tour of Megan's studio. There are photos of her studio that can be clicked on to learn more about Megan's "stuff," such as her Elizabeth Blackwell Woman of Science ruler.

The Judy Moody Website

www.judymoody.com

Judy Moody fans can visit the Judy Moody website to learn all about new Judy Moody and Stink books. There are many fun activities, including games and an art lesson that shows readers how to draw Judy Moody.

Quiz

Q: What is Judy Moody's brother's name?

1

A: Her brother's name is Stink.

Q: How many sisters does Megan have?

2

A: She has four sisters.

Q: What was the first story Megan wrote about?

3

A: Her first story was about a pencil sharpener.

28

Q: Before Megan became a full-time writer, what was her job?

A: She worked in a bookstore and as a librarian.

Q: Where did Megan grow up?

A: She grew up in Pittsburgh, Pennsylvania.

Q: What is Megan's husband's name?

A: Her husband's name is Richard Haynes.

Q: What grade is Judy Moody in?

A: Judy Moody is in the third grade.

Q: What is the name of Megan's first published book?

A: *Is This a House for Hermit Crab?* was Megan's first published book.

Q: When Megan began stuttering, what book inspired her as a child?

A: *Harriet the Spy* inspired Megan.

Q: What is the name of the book co-starring Judy Moody and Stink?

A: The book is called *The Holly Joliday.*

Writing Terms

This glossary will introduce you to some of the main terms in the field of writing. Understanding these common writing terms will allow you to discuss your ideas about books and writing with others.

action: the moving events of a work of fiction

antagonist: the person in the story who opposes the main character

autobiography: a history of a person's life written by that person

biography: a written account of another person's life

character: a person in a story, poem, or play

climax: the most exciting moment or turning point in a story

episode: a short piece of action, or scene, in a story

fiction: stories about characters and events that are not real

foreshadow: hinting at something that is going to happen later in the book

imagery: a written description of a thing or idea that brings an image to mind

narrator: the speaker of the story who relates the events

nonfiction: writing that deals with real people and events

novel: published writing of considerable length that portrays characters within a story

plot: the order of events in a work of fiction

protagonist: the leading character of a story; often a likable character

resolution: the end of the story, when the conflict is settled

scene: a single episode in a story

setting: the place and time in which a work of fiction occurs

theme: an idea that runs throughout a work of fiction

Glossary

centipedes: long worm-like insects that have dozens of tiny legs

classic: something that has been judged over a long period of time to be of good quality

hardcover: a book with a stiff cover compared to paperback books

huckster: a person who sells items at a small shop or door-to-door

inspired: to be encouraged by a person, place, phrase, or thing to do something

library science: the study of libraries and the collection and organization of information

manuscripts: drafts of a story before it is published

professor: a teacher at a university or a college

storyboards: series of drawings, similar to a comic strip, that are used to organize the events in a story; usually used for making a cartoon or a movie

stutter: repeating the first sound of a word over and over when unable to say the entire word or sentence

therapist: a person who helps others by talking about the other person's feelings and experiences

Index

Photo Credits

Every reasonable effort has been made to trace ownership and to obtain permission to reprint copyright material. The publishers would be pleased to have any errors or omissions brought to their attention so that they may be corrected in subsequent printings.

Photo credits: Getty Images: pages 8, 22, 23, 26; Images courtesy of Megan McDonald: pages 1, 3, 7, 9, 10, 11 top, 12, 13, 16, 17; Michele McDonald: page 4; Newscom: page 11 bottom. Pages 18-20: Reproduced by permission of the publisher, Candlewick Press, Inc., Somerville, MA. JUDY MOODY. Text © 2000 Megan McDonald. Illustrations © 2000 Peter Reynolds. JUDY MOODY & STINK: THE HOLLY JOLIDAY. Text copyright © 2007 Megan McDonald. Illustrations copyright © 2007 Peter H. Reynolds. STINK AND THE WORLD'S WORST SUPER-STINKY SNEAKERS. Text copyright © 2007 Megan McDonald. Illustrations copyright © 2007 Peter H. Reynolds. Page 21: © American Girl.